# BOB, ME AND A METAL KNEE

## *A Cycle through Spain*

# BOB, ME AND A METAL KNEE

## *A Cycle through Spain*

To Thelma Bock
x

JOHN SWANKIE

© John Swankie, 2019

Published by The Shooglie Pedal

A CIP catalogue record for this book is available from the British Library.

ISBN 978-1-9996947-0-8

Book layout and cover design by Clare Brayshaw

Prepared and printed by:

York Publishing Services Ltd
64 Hallfield Road
Layerthorpe
York YO31 7ZQ

Tel: 01904 431213

Website: www.yps-publishing.co.uk

# Acknowledgements

'Rich' at Edinburgh Bike Co-op, who made Bob run like a Rolls Royce.

'Nicola' at Redpen, who turned the brickie's grammar into something readable.

'Gilly' who continues to inspire.

'Doddie', just for being Doddie. xx

# Foreword

All proceeds from this book will be evenly divided between My Name'5 Doddie Foundation and the Murrayfield Injured Players Foundation (MIPF):

www.myname5doddie.co.uk
www.mipf.org.uk

When I first mooted my intended cycle trip a few people suggested that I 'do it for charity', but I wasn't comfortable with the idea as I didn't want the inevitable pressure to complete my adventure to a deadline!

I also find it odd to ask for money to do something you ultimately love.

So as usual, I have gone about things in my own way and decided that, having left school at fifteen with no qualifications or scholastic intent but to spend my working life as a bricklayer/builder, writing a book (no matter how short), would be pain enough to allow me the audacity to ask for donations/payment.

As a retired rugby player and long-time supporter of the game, both of the causes I have chosen are close to my heart and worthy of support.

After being diagnosed with MND (Motor Neurone Disease), Doddie has decided to use his celebrity and remaining years to raise funds to help sufferers and hopefully find an eventual cure through research.

MIPF wonderfully ensures that anyone participating in our sport who suffers a life changing injury will be given support and help, as long as needed.

My wish through this small record of my mini adventure is to hopefully add to both funds and help both charities to carry on their good work.

I sincerely hope you enjoy the read and think it was a few quid well spent.

Swankie

P.S. I have, as it turns out, hugely enjoyed the whole experience!

# Plymouth to Santander –
# (The journey begins)

I am standing beside Bob, my bike, in an empty lane facing the back of the enormous ship that will ferry me to Spain, and I have started to feel edgy that, apart from a couple of cars and a motorhome in another lane, I'm alone.

'Be early,' they said, 'as it gets very busy.'

I decided to go for a wander, but at that moment a huge motorbike loaded with panniers and two people onboard glided to a halt beside me. During a ten minute chat about our respective journeys and expectations, an enormous convoy of vehicles and people descended to fill every available space. Around 50 gleaming motorbikes ended up queued behind me, each one seemingly bigger and shinier than the last, but not one other cyclist!

Amidst all the leather-clad noise and fumes I felt a bit conspicuous in baggy shorts and one horsepower transport, so I took myself off to a bench, opened my first bag of Jelly Babies of the tour and adopted 'lonely soldier' status.

A few of the bikers stopped to ask about my trip and seemed both impressed and amused that I had planned to tackle the contours of Spain without 1000cc assistance. A fella from another lane introduced himself and it turned out that he was renting a holiday home for the winter very close to my finish point in Los Alcazares in the Murcia region. He and his wife were driving a small van with necessary gear, including his bike. It turns out that 'Gilly' was ex-military and ran his own business specialising in map reading, nutrition and general survival skills. He had cycled my journey a few times and assured me I would make it no problem.

I probably had not made it clear to Gilly that my fitness may be somewhat less than adequate, and that I have an inbuilt ability to get lost even going to places I've been to before! But I felt uplifted as I was guided into the bowels of the ship and handed a piece of rope to tie Bob up to a rail on the side of the hull.

OK...we set off into the Bay of Biscay and there wasn't much to do for the next thirteen hours, so I have used this time to bring you up to speed.

## The Trip

Santander: Northern Spain.
to
La Puebla: South Eastern Spain.
Distance: 650 miles approximately.
11 days cycling, averaging 60 miles per day.
2 rest days: Burgos and Cuenca.

## The Team

### Jock (me)

Sixty-two year-old builder.
A bit overweight.
Common sense of a 12 year-old, mental capacity of a chicken.
Needed an adventure.

### 'Bob Jackson' (bike)

Was first seen as a frame and forks hanging in my local bike shop.

Made into the comfiest and best bike ever – a friend for life!

### 'Natasha'

A ten year old 'Navigon' Sat Nav bought for £60.00 from Halfords.

Never been updated and sometimes didn't have a 'scooby' but she has a nice voice! And I like bossy women.

### 'Knobby'

My twelve year-old metal replacement knee, who has a wee drug problem; and demands 'Ibuprofen' when under duress.

### Hazel/Mission Control/My Wife

I asked if she could do all the organising and worrying whilst I went off and did something daft. She replied, 'I've been doing that for twenty-eight years. Why ask now?'

I couldn't argue with that one!

As with most of my 'great ideas,' this one came to me on the bike one day and by the time I had gone around Loch Leven and arrived home, it had formed into a plan.

After many years running our small building business, Hazel and I had decided that, whilst unable to 'fully' retire, we could probably manage to create longer gaps between contracts to enjoy some downtime. Therefore, setting aside October to cycle across Spain and meet

Hazel at the other end for a final week's holiday seemed to fit the bill.

I started training during August, with a 50 miler to St Andrews, rough-camped Saturday night on the West Sands and returned home on Sunday, knackered. During September I cycled to Dundee a couple of times to watch the Dunfermline 1stXV rugby lads play. The second time I loaded the bike with the 20lbs of kit I would be carrying through Spain. The rest of my training regime involved twenty to thirty mile Sunday morning rides to bring home the Sunday papers.

As you see, I'm not really big on preparation!

Coincidently, I found a book by a guy who had covered almost the same journey I was proposing, albeit in reverse, which proved useful in planning distances and stopovers.

The boys from the rugby club suggested that I download a running and cycling app called Strava, which allows people to follow your progress, so they would be able to follow me. After some initial squealing and stress, I managed to get the app onto my phone and after some practise found it to be a really great asset. (Welcome to modern life, Jock).

I had a minor equipment disaster when lifting Bob down from his hook in the garage. I managed to snag my precious Gore touring shorts with the front chainring and tear the side of the cargo pocket. After 10 years of amazing service those bad boys were not getting dumped, so after a hasty browse and click on Amazon I was able to send for, and sew on, three patches. It turned out that these made my shorts into a conversation piece and icebreaker when strangers saw a Scottish flag, a Spanish flag and in between them a motto which read:

'Don't let fear and common sense hold you back.'

My pal Linda gave me a cracking journal to fill out daily during the trip, and Hazel booked cycle-friendly accommodation and handed me a full list of instructions for everything!

I cut out several pages from a Spanish road atlas and was ready to rumble.

## DAY ONE

# Santander to Espinosa De Los Monteros

I picked today's destination for two reasons.

1  The ferry docked at noon and I thought approximately 50 miles was achievable before dark.
2  I really liked the name.

It was almost 2pm by the time we had disembarked and cleared customs, but I found it hard to be concerned as I set off in glorious sunshine with 'Natasha' in charge of leading me out of the city. We made it out into open countryside and I guess I should have switched her off but I was enjoying the company.

After a while, and two attempts to guide me onto the new 'Autovia' (motorway) which was very clearly marked 'No biceclatas', I decided to pull out the pages of the map and sort it out. Disappointingly, I had to cycle an hour and a further ten miles, doubling back to get onto the correct road.

On the outskirts of a village called Lierganes, I spotted a fella washing a taxi outside his home and decided he may be the right man to verify that I was now heading in the right direction. So I asked, and obviously my meagre Spanish failed its first test instantly! He was rightly amused by my predicament and asked me to wait a moment before returning with pencil and paper, then drew me a splendidly detailed map of directions and then did something that was to be a recurring theme during my journey. He looked at Bob, then pointed to the sky to alert me of the mountain looming in the distance. We parted friends, my excitement at finally being sure of my route overtook me and I cycled merrily away on the left-hand side of the road, British-style, much to the consternation of the van driver heading towards me. Focus Jock, focus!

I began climbing through beautiful scenery that I would have expected to see in Switzerland rather than Spain, with chalet-style houses dotted around the hillside and cows wearing bells around their necks, wandering freely.

The climbing began in earnest then, with endless switchbacks and cows being replaced by goats clinging to the mountainside. I looked up, hoping to see an end in sight, but in the gathering dusk could only see low cloud above and a ribbon of road in the distance. I eventually reached the summit at ten to eight with the darkness looming. I photographed the sign at the top, 'Portilla Lunada 1350M,' and just as I tried to contact Hazel to let her know all was well, the bloody phone died!

The good news was there was only one road, so I could not possibly get lost, and as this was a summit sign, it must be downhill. OH! What a joy to be right for once, nine miles freewheeling at 20mph in the dull glow of my head torch, both terrifying and exhilarating at the same time.

On arrival at Espinosa De Los Monteros I found my hotel in the centre of town but was surprised to find it in darkness and seemingly closed. After some enthusiastic door hammering, the lady owner appeared and apologised but mentioned that I was a bit late.

She informed me the hotel was under refurbishment and I could store my bike in the currently unused restaurant. This was both good and bad, as Bob was now secure but there was no food available. Having had only breakfast and a bag of Jelly Babies all day, a quick shower and a restaurant were a priority.

After what was a disappointingly freezing cold shower, I descended on the only pub still open in town. They only had 'pinchos,' (small bar snacks) available, so I picked one of everything. Four pinchos, three beers, one coffee and one brandy later, I retired to bed for a well earned sleep.

Unfortunately the bell of the church next to the hotel rang the time every hour, on the hour, all through the night. And just in case you missed it, there was a pause and it rang the time again. Then, as a special surprise it chimed once every half hour.

I lay in bed thinking that if the minister was on the street tomorrow, he would be likely to get a kick in the cloisters!

**The Stats**

Distance – 54 miles
Height climbed – 7,691 feet
Time on bike – 6 hours 21 minutes.

*Can you spot Bob?*

*An Awfy big boat for a wee bike*

*A hell of a climb!*

*Its downhill from here!*

## Day Two

# Espinosa De Los Monteros to Burgos

Panaderia for breakfast, which was one large cheese pastry, two large donuts and a bottle of fizzy juice – one happy endurance athlete!

Navigation was going to be easy this day. I would get on the CL629 and stay on it all the way to Burgos. It was a very cold morning, I had to put on my jacket and tuck my hands behind the bar bag to keep the wind off.

I was very quickly out into open countryside and struck by the sheer scale of the landscape, with the road snaking like a giant roller coaster into the far distance. I was suddenly aware that I was from a small country, one where the surroundings seemed to hug you; indeed, even the sky seemed lower in Scotland.

About twenty miles in I hit the first climb of the day, 'La Mazorra', rising 1000m with switchbacks all the way.

Message to self: when in bottom gear doing 4mph, don't look up to see how far you have to go as tears are a needless waste of water!

Later in the day I saw the longest, straightest downhill stretch of road I have ever seen ahead of me and freewheeled for what seemed miles, at one point reaching 41.8mph without turning a pedal.

I switched 'Natasha' on at the outskirts of Burgos and she took me straight to my hotel door. I guess she is a city girl.

Mission Control had excelled, with a beautiful old hotel bang in the centre of the city. I locked Bob safely behind reception and I headed up to my room which I managed to turn it into a laundry with just-washed kit hanging everywhere. I decided to go in search of food, food, food, and as tomorrow was a day off the bike, I planned to have a drink or two as well.

**The Stats**

Distance – 60.6 miles
Height climbed – 4261 feet
Time on bike – 5 hours 33 mins

*Smooth tar as far as the eye can see*

*Another day, another climb!*

# Day Three

# Burgos

This was my first day off cycling, so I spent it exploring, eating and relaxing.

I washed, dried and packed away all my clothes but I had to source a new bottle of Head & Shoulders as I had used most of it. The upside was that my bum would be dandruff free, courtesy of my clean shorts.

I had spent the day doing touristy stuff; it was good but I felt a bit frustrated by not being on the road. I won't bore you with the cathedrals etc., but I did meet an elderly Australian fella outside a bar, and we had a couple of beers whilst we chatted. It turned out that the 'Camino De Santiago De Compostella' route runs right through Burgos. Apparently it involves thousands of people who travel hundreds of miles on foot, starting in France and ending on the northern tip of Spain. These pilgrims are guided on their way by the sign of a shell marking the route (see photograph of the shell embedded in the pavement and an elderly pilgrim). He was slightly reluctant to be photographed but gave in eventually.

Next I went for 'pollo asado al horno con patatas' (chicken and chips to you and me), then back to the hotel to pack my kit, sleep, breakfast, then hit the road.

*Endurance athlete's diet*

*The weary pilgrim*

*The shell that marks the way*

*A bit of laundry art!*

# Day Four

# Burgos to Aranda De Duera

I had packed up and was ready to go around 8am, with five straight days on the bike ahead until my next rest day in Cuenca. I had no idea what terrain was coming but hoped that the first two days had set me up for the challenge.

It looked like a reasonable 60 miles to Aranda and, as I noticed that 'Natasha' had been set to truck mode, not cycle, I reset her and decided to give her another go.

(Will I never learn?)

We negotiated our exit out of the city perfectly, and for 15 miles or so rolled along at a good pace through open countryside until the A1 Autovia to Madrid cut right across our path. Needless to say, 'Natasha' was enthusiastically encouraging me to join the A1 but the 'No biceclatas' sign was pretty clear.

I ducked into the underpass and went in search of the old road (the one that existed before 'Natasha' was "born") but ended up in an industrial estate on a gravel and sand track, so I retreated and luckily found a small road which took me through a group of houses. I stopped for a think and half a bag of Jelly Babies and decided it was time to get out the pages of the map, but could not find my location. I believe that rule one of finding where you're going is to find out where you are.

I decided a chat to Mission Control was required, and was duly informed that my location as described was on page 17, which was slightly disappointing, as I only had page 18. Oh no! I managed to feign a cheery disposition and informed Hazel of my new plan, which was to 'wing it' along my current road, and allow 'Tash' to eventually guide me to the right road.

I don't think Mission Control's comments would be helpful in print at this stage.

I managed another handful of Jelly Babies and on I went. 'Natasha' kept trying to turn me right onto 'Camino Servico' roads, which may have been tarred at one time but were obviously just gravel tracks to service the fields, so I held out and hoped for better.

I could see I was putting in a lot of miles and time, but making no progress south where I knew my destination Aranda lay, so when I was again urged by 'Natasha' to turn right and there was at least a rough tar surface, I went for it.

I was cycling through vast fields of sunflowers as far as the eye could see, which was difficult as they were as tall as me. It would have been quite stunning had the flowers not all been standing brown and dead, I guessed waiting to be cropped for oil or seeds.

Just to complete a fairly gloomy scene, the tar ran out to leave a very bumpy gravel track, and after about a mile it became unrideable. I looked at 'Natasha' .....just as her light went out. I was all alone!

As the new expedition leader, I had a decision to make. Go back three miles to where I knew I didn't want to be, or walk on in the last direction indicated by 'Natasha' before she deserted me.

I've never been a "go back" kind of guy, so I plodded on.

After about another mile, I spotted a couple of roofs sticking above the sunflowers and reasoned that even if only sheds, nobody got to them this way, so there must be a road out.

I eventually came out of the fields into a small farmstead, to be confronted by two very surprised ladies who were sitting comfortably with a basket between them, dressing vegetables.

Now, I may be wrong, but I think it is probable that I am the first dust-covered Scotsman pushing a bike who has ever burst out of the crops. I decided it was time to deploy the one Spanish phrase I had practised to perfection before leaving home.

'Hola, soy Escoces Y estoy perdido'.

(Hello, I'm Scottish and I am lost).

There was roughly five seconds of silence, and then all three of us fell about laughing.

The problem now was, they thought I could speak Spanish. They began waving arms in all directions and verbally machine gunning me, which largely meant I was still lost.

Amidst all the laughing, waving and shrugging, I saw a wee elderly chap emerge from a farm shed and head over to see what all the fuss was about. Now, I have to admit, to my eternal shame, that I saw a boiler suit, flat cap, fag-end and one tooth and thought, 'No chance!'

He wandered over, looked me and Bob up and down, then entered into a discussion with my new girlfriends. After about a minute he turned to me and with perfect diction asked, 'Do you speak English?' If I hadn't thought he may have shot me, I would have kissed him!

He then went on to give me clear directions to the nearby town of Lerma and onwards to Aranda.

I hugged the three of them and left feeling guilty about my assumption based on appearance, but hugely uplifted by the whole experience.

I can only imagine there was a conversation around the family table that evening that began, 'You'll never guess what happened today?'

On entering Lerma I stopped for a much-needed refuel of beer, tapas and strong coffee. I perused my map and found Lerma on page 18, which meant I was back in the game. But I realised the only road out of town heading to Aranda was the A1 (No biceclatas).

A group of builders were having lunch at a table nearby so I thought I would give my kindred spirits the chance to get me out of trouble. Luckily one of the younger guys had some English, and he explained that there was a gravel service road alongside the main carriageway that may be cycleable, and that after 5km there was a junction that would allow me to take the quieter roads to Aranda.

I arrived at the roundabout on the outskirts of town and decided that I had seen enough gravel for one day, so rode down the slip-road and onto the hard shoulder of the A1 for a 5km sprint, managing to evade arrest, and joined a country road at the next junction.

**The Stats**

Distance – 74.2 miles
Height climbed – 3991 feet
Time – 7.3 hours

*Lost among the sunflowers*

*Another 'Bloody Bell'*

*The shorts of inspiration*

# Day Five

# Aranda to Burgos De Osma

We started out later on day five, as I wanted to give Bob a thorough clean and service after yesterday's off-roading. I had also made new friends the previous night with the family who owned the bar opposite the hotel and they had invited me for breakfast. I have absolutely no idea how that happened as we shared no common language at all, but I guess a Scotsman with a few drinks makes him everyone's pal.

The breakfast feast comprised of: tortilla, pork belly, bread, ham, padron peppers, lots of coffee and lots of Spanish chat (none by me!).

Mucho gracias to my host, 'Dormir Juan Manuel Canelo Yenque'; try saying that with a mouthful of tortilla.

The route that day looked quite short if done directly, so for once I proposed to deviate on purpose to look at a lake, 'Embalse De Linares Del Arroyo', largely to see how it might compare to a Scottish Loch. It did not disappoint.

The lake was very picturesque, with a beautiful arched, stone bridge leading to a monastery perched on a hill. The sun was shining, which made it the perfect place to hang last night's washing on Bob to dry, and for me to catch a few rays.

The ride itself today was fast and straight with no major climbs. 'Natasha' was back in the bag as soon as we cleared the city and 'Knobby' was in a drug induced haze. So all was well, if uninspiring.

Mission Control had excelled herself again and booked me into an awfully posh hotel. Bob was in his own space in the underground garage, and as I entered the foyer it was obvious there was a big wedding on that day. All the Miss World contestants were gathered in reception and, amidst all the shiny suits and general glamour, the dusty bike traveller slunk off to his room.

In my ensuite I was confronted with a vast array of really nice smelling toiletries and immediately decided that these would be much better off living in my panniers for the remainder of the trip.

I'm not sure if my surroundings affected me but I decided to add my 'going ashore' pants to my cycle laundry routine; I figured five evenings of wear put them at their limit.

On the subject of routine I had been writing up my journal every evening, photographing the pages and texting them to Hazel, along with any photographs taken throughout the day. It was only when I was asked to tidy up my writing that I became aware she was posting it on Facebook and I had gone viral with the rugby boys, many friends from all over the world and strangers all sharing my journey...cool!

The other vital part of my evening regime involved yoga stretches, for my lower back and hamstrings. After many years of building work and a bad knee, these areas needed constant management. The single most important bit of kit in my bag was my stretching band. This was a long strap with loops along its length, which allowed me a gentle stretching of tight 'hammies' and worked brilliantly.

## The Stats

Distance – 57.4 miles
Height climbed – 2734 feet
Time – 5.07 hours

*Bob drying our kit*

# Day Six

## Burgos De Osma to Sigunza

I woke up a bit grizzly this morning as some numpty had been doing the bloody bell thing again, all night.

I was beginning to regret asking Hazel to ensure my hotels were within walking distance of the town centre. I now realised that all Spanish towns grow up around a big church and employ enthusiastic, insomniac monks to man the bell tower nightly. Anyway, I got up and got ready to put on my dinner jacket and join the wedding party for breakfast.

The ride to Siguenza turned out to be really tough today, with a long, lumpy road. The wind had been strong against me all day and it was just a case of head down and get it done.

This area is the least populated in Spain and supplies were hard to find. The hot wind seemed to be drawing the moisture out of me and I was thirsty all day. Everything was hurting, even bits I've not given a name to, and those arrow- straight roads that stretched for miles into the distance became very difficult to reel in.

A combine harvester passed me and I instinctively put the hammer down and tucked in behind him, which gave me a magical twenty minutes of easy riding until he turned off.

I was getting desperate for water and food, so I targeted a village on the map about five miles up the road to re-supply. On arrival at the only pub in town I spotted a road bike, loaded with frame and seat packs, leaning outside. Since boarding the ferry at Plymouth I had not encountered a single tour cyclist, so I was well chuffed to find a Kiwi all the way from Christchurch, sitting in the corner of the bar. We shared a couple of beers, some food and a good chat, but we both had miles to do and sadly soon went our separate ways, both happy to have met someone who almost spoke English.

I rode on through the endless fields of sunflowers and could only imagine how spectacular a sight it would have been in full bloom but sadly, as before, they stood withered and brown; thankfully though, the road was tarmac.

As I rolled down into Sigunza I spotted a very big, beautiful cathedral; the next day was Sunday. I contemplated climbing the tower and wrapping my spare pants around the bell as an act of sabotage.

**The Stats**

Distance – 65.9 miles
Height climbed – 3524 feet
Time – 5 hours 47 mins

# Day Seven

## Sigunza to Sacedon

I had hoped for an easier test today and it started really well. There had been no nighttime bell and I left before the sinners were called to church in the morning.

I had a couple of steep climbs early on but they were mostly short 'ups' with long 'downs'. With the wind at my back and the sun on my face, I thought I had cracked it.

Then the 'A' road turned up. I could see my old friend, 'Camino Servico' so jumped on and came out onto a road that should have been mine, but after five miles I began to get edgy when town names on the road signs didn't correspond with my map page.

I cycled into a small 'Barrio', (small village) and although I could see the church tower of where I wanted to be in the distance, a fella told me I would have to backtrack to the main road and cycle around five miles back to the junction I had obviously missed. That would have meant pedalling into the wind and cycling miles already covered, so the impetuous youth that I am I decided to 'wing it' and hammer down the road I was on, even though it took me off the map page I had with me, but I felt lucky.

Ten miles further on I rolled down a steep hill into a town and asked for help.

The good news was I could reach Sacedon on this road but this fella kept looking at Bob and me, then pointed to the sky and shook his head. This was a phenomenon I was encountering frequently during my tour and it appeared to be the standard way of warning the ageing, non-Spanish-speaking cyclist of an impending mountain. This was always followed by a hearty slap on the back, a wide smile and a 'Buenos suerte', to send you on your way.

The particular mountain that afternoon was indeed a lump, but my legs were getting noticeably stronger as the trip progressed, so it was no big deal.

I rode into town after sixty miles at around 4.30pm, having eaten a continental breakfast and an apple all day. I urgently needed fuel and a drink, so had my heart set on 'menu del dia' (menu of the day) at the first restaurant in town. This was one of General Franco's better ideas, whereby every Spaniard is able to afford one cooked meal a day. This consists generally of bread, salad, a main course of fish or meat, vegetables, dessert and a drink.

Now, when you are hungry and tired with a specific heartfelt desire, it makes for a particularly crushing blow when 'Mr Grumpy' the restaurateur points at a sign saying: 'Menu de Dia terminado 4pm', then walks away...

My post-ride lunch was spent in the town's Rehpsol petrol station and consisted of 1 x ham sandwich, 1 x tube Pringles, 1 x Snickers bar, 1 x bag of peanut M&M's and one large bottle of water. All gone in sixty seconds.

Unfortunately this set the tone for a fairly disappointing visit.

I found my hotel and secured Bob in the cellar of the bar/cafe opposite; this was also where breakfast was served in the morning. I then returned to my room to sort out my kit. The map pages and hotel booking forms were in a bit of disarray in my bar bag so I decided to tidy and file them. You may remember that on day four my lack of page 17 led to all sorts of bother, so you can imagine my surprise to discover during my tidy that page 17 was actually on the reverse side of page 18...d'oh! Who could have guessed that, right?!

I went to the hotel restaurant to eat but the food was very poor, so wandered to the bar across the square in search of a beer and a friendly face, but I only found the beer.

I guess I had just hit a bit of a low and was back in 'lonely soldier' mode when I received some text banter from my son, Scott and son-in-law, Tam, based around the obvious failings in my map reading and the effect of cross winds on my big nose.

I went to bed laughing. I decided that I had better phone my kayak pal, Kenneth, at some point to report my page 17 debacle, as he would find it both funny and recognisable; Kenneth has been a victim of my tour guidance before.

**The Stats**

Distance − 62.2 miles
Height climbed − 3624 feet
Time − 5 hours 33 minutes

## Day Eight

# Sacedon to Cuenza

I got up good to go and went across to the cafe for breakfast and to retrieve Bob from the cellar.

This was a proper local haunt, so I decided to go for the (almost) full Spanish breakfast of tostada (toast) and tomato puree, olive oil, salt, strong coffee and orange juice. I say almost full Spanish because I had foregone the large Spanish brandy everyone else had finished off with, including the four Guarda Civil officers seated at the bar with the patrol cars tucked away up the alley behind the cafe 8.30am...let's get the party started!

So on to Cuenza and a rest day.

Around fifty miles of main road all the way with sign posts, no maps and no bother; would I make it before 4pm? You betcha! I was around a quarter of a mile in and hit a killer climb that went on forever. I don't think the Ibuprofen had kicked in because 'Knobby' was really sore and very tight all the way up. But we grizzled our way to the top and flew off what felt like the end of the world at over 40mph and the freewheeling just kept going.

The most worrying things on the main roads were the big trucks because they generated a lot of wind power and, although the hard shoulder was wide and cyclists were fairly separated from the traffic, you needed to focus to keep a straight line.

There was one big climb to come and the sign at the bottom stated 15%. I did not know what a 15% incline was like, but after three miles of out of the seat pedalling, I now do.

As I was going over the top a big truck passed and the driver put on his hazard lights, blew his horn and waved. I thought that was cool!

The last ten miles into Cuenza were like a magic carpet of smooth tar; ever-so-slightly sloping downwards and instigating a full, top-gear sprint finish.

Did I make 'menu del dia?'

Ooooh...yes!

Paella, pork and roast potatoes with a fried egg, followed by meringue tart, beer and coffee all for €10... Viva Espania!!

I was very glad I was refuelled down in the main city as my hotel was a near- vertical walk of around a mile through narrow, cobbled streets, but Mission Control had excelled yet again. I was encamped in the heart of the hilltop citadel and World Heritage site. The next day was a day off the bike and I planned to become a Michael Palin-esque explorer.

**The Stats**

Distance – 50.9 miles
Height climbed – 3398 feet
Time – 4 hours 43 mins.

# Day Nine

## Cuenca

This mountaintop fortress was started by the Romans and fought over by Arabs, Moors and Christian Crusaders and most recently General Franco.

It is very difficult to attack because of the ravines around it and can only be won by siege and starvation.

It is a wee bit like my home town of Inverkeithing really.

I do not really have the words to describe the drama and the beauty of this place, with the houses hanging from the cliffs and beautiful buildings everywhere. Whilst visiting the cathedral I sneaked into an empty chapel and recorded myself singing, and I can only say the acoustics helped a lot.

As I walked around the magnificent town and craned my neck to see the top of the houses that hugged the cliffside, I decided that I would come back here with Mission Control, aka Hazel, at a later date for sure.

The next day I was scheduled to head for Belmonte. I was going to have to cycle down the cobbles and hoped they wouldn't shoogle all the gear off my bike.

*The hills have eyes!*

*Don't invite a crowd to your balcony party!*

*Amazing*

*The accoustics are great*

## Day Ten

# Cuenza to Belmonte

I wanted to get on the road early as I had planned a detour onto quieter back roads so that I could look at some lakes. Unfortunately I got trapped by a fella at breakfast who spent twenty minutes telling me all about the places he and his three mates had visited since leaving Santander, which included Burgos and Cuenza. Twenty minutes...really?

When he stopped for breath I very quickly ran through where I had visited and where I had yet to go, then headed for reception. As I walked away he said; 'So you're just taking small, easy days then?' I laughed and shrugged my shoulders in agreement.

I was across the street loading up Bob when he and his mates came out to retrieve their motorbikes from the hotel garage and, on seeing me, said 'Bloody hell, you never said you were on a push bike!'

'Oh, didn't I?' said the ever-so-slightly smug cyclist. I know it was wrong but it felt good.

I negotiated my way out of the city easily enough and felt really strong after my rest day, so went looking for country roads, hills and lakes and it made for a great day on the bike.

Even the rainy bits did not spoil it as it gave Bob and I a chance to wear our matching hi vis wet gear for half an hour.

On a fast downhill run through a forest I heard a sudden horrible screeching and thought Bob had suffered a mechanical catastrophe, so I stopped immediately. Strangely, the screeching continued and I realised it was coming from the woods beside us. Bob and I looked at each other and then high-tailed it out of there 'mucho pronto'. I can only imagine some beastie was being eaten and didn't like it.

We made it safely to Belmonte too late for big eats, so settled for a couple of beers before finding our hotel. What a hotel it was.

I spent the night in a 17th century 'Palacio' and it was beautiful. I decided not to bother with the town but whiled away the evening strolling through the hotel and grounds. I hugged seven hundred year-old stone columns, and stroked very old, dark wood beams and banisters. Sad I know, but awfully pleasing to the lonely builder on a bike.

I had a glorious meal and a superb Rioja but here is the best bit: 'a cafe Belmonte' is a special coffee of the Murcia region which Hazel and I love and consists of a glass with condensed milk in the bottom, a large shot of strong coffee and an equally large shot of brandy. Just stir and enjoy.

I had asked for one at every stop from Santander only to receive blank looks but this place was called Belmonte, so surely?

Well, I asked and just for a moment I thought I had joined the Masons. The waiter tapped the side of his nose conspiringly and whispered 'I make a very special señor'. Do you know what? He bloody well did. Apparently heating the brandy with your cigarette lighter before pouring is the secret and that made it the best I have had. I slept like a king.

## The Stats

Distance – 74.5 miles
Height climbed – 1174 feet
Time – 6 hours 7 minutes

*Bob and me break out the wet gear!*

*At last*

*A very special 'Belmonte'*

## DAY ELEVEN

# Belmonte to Albacete

The landscape now changed; the roads were absolutely arrow-straight and flat, with huge juggernauts hurtling past at high speeds. There were vast fields with large scale agriculture and huge industrial estates on the outskirts of every town. In short, modern life had infiltrated, so not a lot to tell really, apart from my first crash of the journey, which made for an interesting interlude.

I was freewheeling at around 20mph through a large town, keeping pace with the traffic flowing outside of me on my left. There was a row of cars parked nose to the kerb on my right, when a people carrier swung right in front of me into a parking slot but didn't make it all the way. I had no chance of stopping a fully loaded Bob so instinctively turned my wheel and took the hit with my shoulder.

It all happened in the blink of an eye and, although shaken, I checked Bob and myself over. As I did so, a very angry driver left his car hanging half in the space and blocking the traffic to come round and shout at me. If this guy did not know what an angry Scotsman sounds like, he does now. I guess there are some words that are internationally recognisable as he took a slight step back just as the driver next to us came out and started berating him also. Arms were waving and things were heated, and when I looked over the angry Spaniard's shoulder I could see a slight 'me' shaped depression in the panel of his motor, so I hopped onto Bob and pedalled off. A hundred yards up the road I looked back and could still see waving arms amidst the traffic so I slipped quietly on my way.

I found my hotel in the city centre and after the usual sorting out of my things went in search of food and drink.

I found both in abundance in the large city centre and ended up in a heavy rock bar of all things, which is not my scene. Three things should have alerted me to the fact I was a wee bit drunk:

1. I asked the barman if they could play some Willie Nelson.
2. I tried to play 'Name That Tune' with my old pal Joe over the phone (he wasn't that keen).
3. I attempted to find my hotel using Google maps and failed as I was walking away from the dot, not following it...enough said.

**The Stats**

Distance – 74.5 miles
Height climbed – 1174 feet
Time – 6 hours 7 minutes

# Day Twelve

# Albacete to Cieza

I decided to give 'Natasha' one more chance and keyed in the town name on the road I wanted and left it to her to get us out of town. I must have burned three miles going in a circle, and when I passed the same lady sitting having breakfast outside a cafe for the third time, I knew I had to try something different. I switched 'Natasha' off for a few minutes then turned her back on, apologised for all the harsh words I had used recently and, ten minutes later, was rolling along the road I needed.

I guess sometimes you just have to work at a relationship, huh!

The road I wanted to attempt this day ran beside and played hide-and-seek with the A30 to Murcia (No biceclatas) and I have to say, it was amazing. Apart from a few cars around the villages I was the lonesome cowboy on a superb two-lane road, as everyone else was on the Autovia. It was surreal and made for fantastic time, with fairly flat terrain and great views of the next day's mountains looming in the distance.

Cieza turned out to be a smashing town where families gathered in the main square to eat ice cream, walk, chat and enjoy the company.

It was heartwarming but lonely at the same time; still, there was only one more day to go.

**The Stats**

Distance – 64.7 miles
Height climbed – 2068 feet
Time – 5 hours

# Day Thirteen

## Cieza to La Puebla

I found myself up and ready very early and surprised at my eagerness to complete my journey.

My plan was to follow the 'Rio Segura' valley through the 'Sierra Ricote' as far as Murcia and then 'wing it'. If I had stopped for every photo opportunity along my route I would still be out there as it was simply stunning.

I cycled a beautiful, meandering road which followed the river down through small lakes surrounded by palm trees and olive groves. There was an amazing reservoir with an impressive dam and rural Spain returned in all its glory.

Then, on the last day as on the first, I took a wrong turn and turned an easy sixty-miler with one mountain range into an eighty-miler with two mountains, but after two weeks on the road Bob and I just laughed and my legs just kept on spinning.

I ended up cycling through a glorious National Park a long way west of my destination and, with a mixture of fatigue and devilment, cycled the last twenty-five miles on an 'A' road and, apart from a few horn blasts, I again managed to avoid arrest. I rested Bob against the 'La Puebla' sign for one last photograph, then pedalled the last wee bit to see if Hazel would make me 'menu del dia'...Ha Ha!

**The Stats**

Distance – 79.4 miles
Height climbed – 3625 feet
Time – 7 hours 7 mins

*The beautiful Segura Valley*

*An extra bump due to me being lost 'again'*

# Jock's Tour de Espania –
# The Final Word

When I decided to make this journey it was, as ever with me, 'just because'. I am sure any knee surgeon would have strongly advised against it.

So, it is lucky I never asked one.

I have seen a very narrow strip of Spain, from the rural north, where the cows with bells wander freely and goats cling to the mountainside, down through the plains of 'La Mancha' to the big scale agriculture and industry of the heartland, and finally the coast, with its tourist urbanisations alongside traditional sleepy towns.

I have seen castles, cathedrals and stunning rocky peaks, but the truth is, apart from almost constant sunshine, olive groves and a few palm trees, it's an awful lot like Scotland.

It sometimes is just the sheer scale of the landscape that makes you stop and stare.

The people, just like us, are too busy getting on with life to notice the daft Scots boy on the bike, but ask for help and, just like us they will stop what they are doing, try to show you the way then cheerfully point out the mountain in the distance and wish you 'Buenos suerte'

I wrote down some rules for the trip on the back page of my journal a few months ago and, apart from pedalling sometimes just for the sheer joy of it, I have stuck to them.

Especially the getting lost one.
You can read them below.

## The Total Stats

Distance = 709.5 miles
Height climbed = 39,851 feet
Time on bike = 63 hours 33 minutes
Average speed = 10.9 mph

## Does any of this make me a 'cyclist'?

Nah, cyclists fly past me every day wearing heart rate monitors and worrying about their VO2 max.

I'm just a fella with a bike who likes a wee adventure.

Until the next time –

Hasta luego xx

*Journey's End*

*The lonely soldier, home!*

# Rules of the Tour

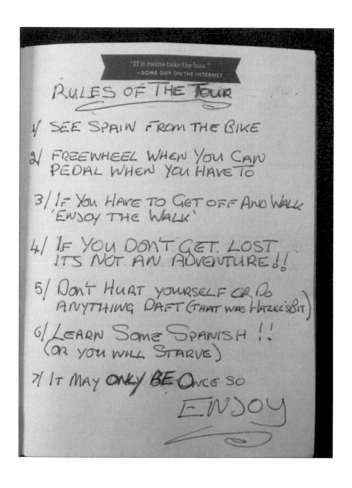

"If it rains take the bus."
— SOME GUY ON THE INTERNET

RULES OF THE TOUR

1/ SEE SPAIN FROM THE BIKE

2/ FREEWHEEL WHEN YOU CAN
PEDAL WHEN YOU HAVE TO

3/ IF YOU HAVE TO GET OFF AND WALK
'ENJOY THE WALK'

4/ IF YOU DON'T GET. LOST
ITS NOT AN ADVENTURE!!

5/ DON'T HURT YOURSELF OR DO
ANYTHING DAFT (THAT WAS HAZEL'S BIT)

6/ LEARN SOME SPANISH !!
(OR YOU WILL STARVE)

7/ IT MAY ONLY BE ONCE SO
ENJOY